# EVERYTHING Beautiful

A COLORING BOOK FOR REFLECTION AND INSPIRATION

WATERBROOK

EVERYTHING BEAUTIFUL

All Scripture quotations, unless otherwise indicated, are taken from the Holy Bible, New International Version®, NIV®. Copyright © 1973, 1978, 1984 by Biblica Inc.® Used by permission. All rights reserved worldwide. Scripture quotations marked (ESV) are taken from the ESV® Bible (the Holy Bible, English Standard Version®), copyright © 2001 by Crossway, a publishing ministry of Good News Publishers. Used by permission. All rights reserved. Scripture quotations marked (MSG) are taken from the Message. Copyright © by Eugene H. Peterson 1993, 1994, 1995, 1996, 2000, 2001, 2002. Used by permission of Tyndale House Publishers Inc.

Lyrics from "Needle and Thread" written by Ryan O'Neal © 2006, Wine and Song Music (BMI) on behalf of itself and Asteroid B-612. International copyright secured. All rights reserved. Used by permission. Lyrics from "How Great Thou Art" © 1949 and 1953 by the Stuart Hine Trust. United States of America print rights administered by Hope Publishing Company. All other hymns quoted are in the public domain.

Trade Paperback ISBN 978-0-7352-8981-9

Copyright © 2016 by WATERBROOK

Cover design by Kristopher K. Orr; cover image by Jennifer Tucker

Published in the United States by WaterBrook, an imprint of the Crown Publishing Group, a division of Penguin Random House LLC, New York.

WATERBROOK® and its deer colophon are registered trademarks of Penguin Random House LLC.

Printed in the United States of America
2016—First Edition

10 9 8 7 6 5 4 3 2 1

SPECIAL SALES
Most WaterBrook books are available at special quantity discounts when purchased in bulk by corporations, organizations, and special-interest groups. Custom imprinting or excerpting can also be done to fit special needs. For information, please e-mail specialmarketscms@penguinrandomhouse.com or call 1-800-603-7051.

# Find Beauty Everywhere

*Life is beautiful.*

We say it all the time. Our Instagram feeds are full of picturesque scenes where the light shines just perfectly so our go-to filter makes our surroundings look like they came from something out of a Tolkien novel. We talk to our coworkers about our beautiful adventures outside of work, we tell the most adorable stories of our children, and we make sure we humblebrag about the sweet, romantic gesture our husbands made last weekend.

But no one sees the fight you two had before he got you those flowers. No one sees you losing your temper after your kids kept banging on the bathroom door asking for a snack—because apparently using the bathroom in peace is an outrageous request. No one sees how hard you fought to get out of bed under the crushing weight of depression, and no one is there to watch you try to picture your life after a terrifying diagnosis. When the entire world seems to be embroiled in war, injustice, and disease, it can be hard to see real beauty anywhere—despite the perfect image we curate online.

We live on an unwell earth, and each moment of brokenness only serves to remind us of that fact. Any attempt at finding hope, beauty, or anything remotely good to cling to can sometimes feel like an impossible task. But you and I serve a big God. We serve a God who can't be held back by what ails this earth. We serve a God who promises to give us "a crown of beauty instead of ashes" (Isaiah 61:3).

Our God is one who redeems.

Still, in the midst of the brokenness of this world, that can be hard to remember. The hope for this book is that, as you color and meditate on the words, you are gently reminded of the beauty that can still be found in the bleakest of moments and that this book becomes a bit of a lifeline to remind you our Savior is always there with us. We also hope this book reminds you He has the power to redeem every moment of our lives. Yes, this world is broken, but our Jesus is not.

Music can often express our feelings better than mere words, which is why we created a Spotify playlist called "Everything Beautiful," for which you'll find a link in the back of the book. Play the music while you color, play it on your morning commute, play it when you're feeling trapped in darkness, or simply play it whenever you need to be reminded of the beauty Christ has made from the ashes of this earth.

Of course, it can be easiest to revel in the beauty of this earth when we're spending time with those we love. Grab a group of friends, pop on the playlist, and be reminded of Christ's goodness in a new way. We'd love for you to talk about your coloring adventures on social media too; use the hashtag #EverythingBeautifulBook to join the conversation.

*Everything Beautiful* is about finding beauty in the everyday, the mundane, the broken, and the scary. May this book and the phrases from hymns, scriptures, preachers, teachers, and writers remind you that our God is good, our God is Redeemer, our God loves us, and our God has made everything beautiful.

#EverythingBeautifulBook

"He has made everything beautiful in its time. He has also set eternity in the hearts of men; yet they cannot fathom what God has done from beginning to end." —Ecclesiastes 3:11

Illustrated and hand-lettered by Laura Elizabeth Marshall

## Dare to Be Brave
### by Wilhelmina L. Rooper

Dare to be brave, dare to be true;
Strive for the right, for the Lord is with you;
Fight with sin bravely, fight and be strong;
Christ is your captain; fear only what's wrong.

*Refrain*

*Fight then, good soldiers, fight and be brave;*
*Christ is your captain, mighty to save.*

Dare to be brave, dare to be true,
Hearken to conscience, 'tis God's voice in you;
Though comrades deride and leave you forlorn,
Stand like the hero, unshaken by scorn.

*Refrain*

Dare to be brave, dare to be true;
God is your Father: He watches o'er you;
He knows your trials; when your heart quails,
Call Him to rescue, His grace never fails.

*Refrain*

Dare to be brave, dare to be true,
Shun all dishonor, no mean action do;

Bear pain if it comes, with firmness endure,
Hold to your honor, keep your heart pure.

*Refrain*

Dare to be brave, dare to be true;
Keep the straight way of duty ever in view;
Do all your work as well as you can,
Work for the Lord, not only for man.

*Refrain*

Dare to be brave, dare to be true;
God grant you courage to carry you through;
Try to help others, ever be kind;
Let the oppressed a strong friend in you find.

*Refrain*

Dare to be brave, dare to be true,
Think of the home that's waiting for you;
Home where the faithful whose battles are o'er
Rest in the Lord in joy evermore.

*Refrain*

Wilhelmina L. Rooper penned this hymn in 1889.

Illustrated and hand-lettered by Cari Logston

"I am trying, and will be trying every day for the rest of my life, to look for lovely in the simplest places and the grandest moments. But I'm not always succeeding. I'm that guy on the football team who rarely catches a pass, but the team likes him because he still shows up for practice every day."
—From *Looking for Lovely* by Annie F. Downs (Nashville: B&H, 2016), 179

Annie F. Downs is an author, speaker, and blogger who uses her writing to highlight the everyday goodness of a real and present God. Read her blog at AnnieFDowns.com.

Illustrated and hand-lettered by Jennifer Tucker

Now faith is being sure of what we hope for and certain of what we do not see.

Hebrews 11:1

"Now faith is being sure of what we hope for and certain of what we do not see." —Hebrews 11:1

Illustrated and hand-lettered by Holly Camp

The best and most beautiful THINGS IN THE WORLD cannot be seen or even touched. THEY MUST BE FELT with the HEART.

—HELEN KELLER

"The best and most beautiful things in the world cannot be seen or even touched. They must be felt with the heart." —Helen Keller

Although an unknown illness robbed Helen Keller (1880–1968) of her sight and hearing at nineteen months of age, she refused to let her adversities define her. With the help and dedication of her teacher Anne Sullivan, Helen overcame her childhood rage and her inability to communicate. She went on to earn a college degree and later became an educator and a leading humanitarian, advocating for others with disabilities and bringing encouragement to millions.

Illustrated and hand-lettered by Cari Logston

TO **love** AT ALL IS TO BE VULNERABLE.

♥ C. S. LEWIS ♥

"To love at all is to be vulnerable. Love anything, and your heart will certainly be wrung and possibly be broken. If you want to make sure of keeping it intact, you must give your heart to no one, not even to an animal. Wrap it carefully round with hobbies and little luxuries; avoid all entanglements; lock it up safe in the casket or coffin of your selfishness. But in that casket—safe, dark, motionless, airless—it will change. It will not be broken; it will become unbreakable, impenetrable, irredeemable. The alternative to tragedy, or at least to the risk of tragedy, is damnation. The only place outside Heaven where you can be perfectly safe from all the dangers and perturbations of love is Hell."
—From *The Four Loves* by C. S. Lewis (New York: Harcourt, Brace, Jovanovich, 1960), 169

C. S. Lewis (1898–1963) is considered by many to be one of the top Christian apologists of his time. He authored more than thirty books, including such classics as *Mere Christianity, The Screwtape Letters,* and The Chronicles of Narnia.

Illustrated and hand-lettered by Ann-Margret Hovsepian

We have this hope as an anchor for the soul, firm and secure. —Hebrews 6:19

Hope

"When God made his promise to Abraham, since there was no one greater for him to swear by, he swore by himself, saying, 'I will surely bless you and give you many descendants.' And so after waiting patiently, Abraham received what was promised.

"Men swear by someone greater than themselves, and the oath confirms what is said and puts an end to all argument. Because God wanted to make the unchanging nature of his purpose very clear to the heirs of what was promised, he confirmed it with an oath. God did this so that, by two unchangeable things in which it is impossible for God to lie, we who have fled to take hold of the hope offered to us may be greatly encouraged. We have this hope as an anchor for the soul, firm and secure. It enters the inner sanctuary behind the curtain, where Jesus, who went before us, has entered on our behalf. He has become a high priest forever, in the order of Melchizedek." —Hebrews 6:13–20

Illustrated by Katherine Howe

I NEED TO
CELEBRATE
THE PROGRESS—
NOT THAT I'VE
ARRIVED, BUT THAT
I'M STILL TRYING.

SHAUNA NIEQUIST

"I keep trying, keep trying, keep trying.

"And I think in the midst of all the trying, sometimes I need to celebrate the progress—*not that I've arrived, but that I'm still trying.*" —Shauna Niequist

Shauna Niequist is the author of *Present Over Perfect, Savor, Bread & Wine, Bittersweet,* and *Cold Tangerines.* She writes for the "Storyline" blog and for IF:Table, she is a member of the *Relevant* podcast, and she is a guest teacher at her church.

Illustrated by Jenny Stewart

"Let us acknowledge the LORD;
    let us press on to acknowledge him.
As surely as the sun rises,
    he will appear;
he will come to us like the winter rains,
    like the spring rains that water the earth." —Hosea 6:3

Illustrated by Lisa Shirk

"In all ranks of life the human heart yearns for the beautiful; and the beautiful things that God makes are his gift to all alike." —Harriet Beecher Stowe

Abolitionist Harriet Beecher Stowe (1811–1896) authored the antislavery book *Uncle Tom's Cabin.* Raised in a family that was committed to social justice, Harriet was the seventh of thirteen children of the Reverend Lyman Beecher, a Congregational minister and moral reformer.

Illustrated and hand-lettered by Terra Cypher

"I will exalt you, O Lord,
    for you lifted me out of the depths
and did not let my enemies gloat over me.
    O Lord my God, I called to you for help
    and you healed me.
O Lord, you brought me up from the grave;
    you spared me from going down into the pit.

Sing to the Lord, you saints of his;
    praise his holy name.
For his anger lasts only a moment,
    but his favor lasts a lifetime;
weeping may remain for a night,
    but rejoicing comes in the morning.
When I felt secure, I said,
    'I will never be shaken.'
O Lord, when you favored me,
    you made my mountain stand firm;
but when you hid your face,
    I was dismayed.

To you, O Lord, I called;
    to the Lord I cried for mercy:
'What gain is there in my destruction,
    in my going down into the pit?
Will the dust praise you?
    Will it proclaim your faithfulness?
Hear, O Lord, and be merciful to me;
    O Lord, be my help.'

You turned my wailing into dancing;
    you removed my sackcloth and clothed me with joy,
that my heart may sing to you and not be silent.
    O Lord my God, I will give you thanks forever." —Psalm 30:1–12

Illustrated and hand-lettered by Laura Elizabeth Marshall

## Holy, Holy, Holy
### by Reginald Heber

Holy, holy, holy! Lord God Almighty!
Early in the morning our song shall rise to Thee;
Holy, holy, holy, merciful and mighty!
God in three Persons, blessed Trinity!

Holy, holy, holy! All the saints adore Thee,
Casting down their golden crowns around the glassy sea;
Cherubim and seraphim falling down before Thee,
Who was, and is, and evermore shalt be.

Holy, holy, holy! though the darkness hide Thee,
Though the eye of sinful man Thy glory may not see;
Only Thou art holy; there is none beside Thee,
Perfect in power, in love, and purity.

Holy, holy, holy! Lord God Almighty!
All Thy works shall praise Thy name, in earth, and sky, and sea;
Holy, holy, holy; merciful and mighty!
God in three Persons, blessed Trinity!

Reginald Heber wrote a total of fifty-seven hymns, most of which are still sung today.
"Holy, Holy, Holy," considered his most majestic hymn, was written in 1826 for Trinity
Sunday while he was Vicar of Hodnet, Shropshire, England.

Illustrated and hand-lettered by Lisa Shirk

"Blessed is the man who perseveres under trial, because when he has stood the test, he will receive the crown of life that God has promised to those who love him.

"When tempted, no one should say, 'God is tempting me.' For God cannot be tempted by evil, nor does he tempt anyone; but each one is tempted when, by his own evil desire, he is dragged away and enticed. Then, after desire has conceived, it gives birth to sin; and sin, when it is full-grown, gives birth to death.

"Don't be deceived, my dear brothers. Every good and perfect gift is from above, coming down from the Father of the heavenly lights, who does not change like shifting shadows. He chose to give us birth through the word of truth, that we might be a kind of firstfruits of all he created." —James 1:12–18

Illustrated by Jenny Stewart

Since *love* grows within you, so *beauty grows.* For *love* is the *beauty* of the *soul.*

—SAINT AUGUSTINE

"Since love grows within you, so beauty grows. For love is the beauty of the soul." —Saint Augustine of Hippo

Philosopher, theologian, bishop, and a Latin father of the church, Saint Augustine (AD 354–430) adapted classical thought to Christian teaching and is considered one of the great thinkers in Western Christianity.

Illustrated by Cari Logston

"'Fear not, O Zion;
    let not your hands grow weak.
The LORD your God is in your midst,
    a mighty one who will save;
he will rejoice over you with gladness;
    he will quiet you by his love;
he will exult over you with loud singing.
I will gather those of you who mourn for the festival,
    so that you will no longer suffer reproach.
Behold, at that time I will deal
    with all your oppressors.
And I will save the lame
    and gather the outcast,
and I will change their shame into praise
    and renown in all the earth.
At that time I will bring you in,
    at the time when I gather you together;
for I will make you renowned and praised
    among all the peoples of the earth,
when I restore your fortunes
    before your eyes,' says the LORD." —Zephaniah 3:16–20 (ESV)

Illustrated by Katherine Howe

Beautiful is a million little moments.

—DR. KELLY FLANAGAN

"Beautiful is the stuff that reaches right in, puts electrical paddles on our heart, and shocks us back to life. It's the stuff that wakes us up. It's the stuff that makes us good-ache, like easing off stiff shoes after hours on our feet. It's the stuff that quenches.

"Beautiful is a million little moments." —Dr. Kelly Flanagan, from the blog post "Don't Try to Make Your Life Better (Try to Make It Beautiful-er)," February 17, 2016, at DrKellyFlanagan.com

Dr. Kelly Flanagan is a clinical psychologist and writer. His blog, *UnTangled,* is a place to explore the redemptive life.

Illustrated and hand-lettered by Jennifer Tucker

"When I in awesome wonder
Consider all the worlds thy hands have made…"
—Stuart K. Hine

Stuart K. Hine, an English missionary in Poland in the 1920s, heard a poem titled "O Store Gud" set to a Swedish melody. The lyrics, written by Carl G. Boberg, were in Russian. Hine later wrote his own English version of the poem and composed his own melody, which became "How Great Thou Art."

Illustrated and hand-lettered by Lisa Shirk

"We accept the love we think we deserve."

"Those words weren't just scrawled on a bathroom wall; they're written all over the walls of my heart.

"They were a timely reminder of the truth I've been completely loved before I could even try to deserve it.

"They remind me of the way that Grace overcame my guilt and my striving, my need to prove to earn, to improve.

"They return me to a love that heals and cleanses and satisfies, that overflows into how I live and love and grow.

"They tell me that I don't need to look back.

"That was then. Grace is now." —Jo Saxton, from the blog post "We Accept the Love We Think We Deserve," February 25, 2016, at JoSaxton.com

Jo Saxton is a pastor, speaker, teacher, and author who is passionate about seeing people discover how Jesus transforms our lives and gives our lives purpose.

Illustrated by Jenny Stewart

"Your steadfast love, O Lord, extends to the heavens,
   your faithfulness to the clouds.
Your righteousness is like the mountains of God;
   your judgments are like the great deep;
   man and beast you save, O Lord." —Psalm 36:5–6 (ESV)

Illustrated and hand-lettered by Holly Camp

"I could more easily contain Niagara Falls in a teacup than I can comprehend the wild, uncontainable love of God." —From *The Ragamuffin Gospel* by Brennan Manning, (Colorado Springs: Multnomah, 2005), 153

Former Franciscan priest, evangelist, and best-selling author Brennan Manning (1934–2013) is best known for his books *The Ragamuffin Gospel* and *Abba's Child*. Brennan had a powerful influence on many artists, including DC Talk, Bono, and Rich Mullins. His life mission was "encouraging men and women everywhere to accept and embrace the good news of God's unconditional love in Jesus Christ."

Illustrated and hand-lettered by Terra Cypher

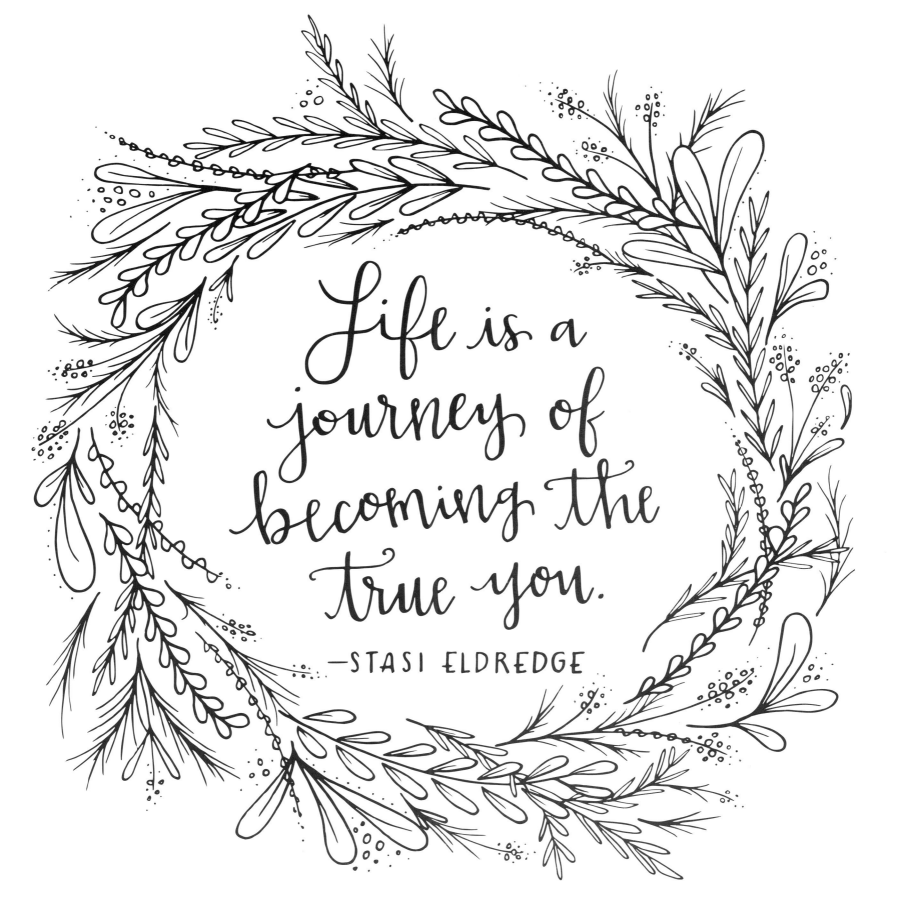

Life is a journey of becoming the true you.

—STASI ELDREDGE

"Life is a journey of becoming the true you."
—From *Free to Be Me* by Stasi Eldredge
(Colorado Springs: David C Cook, 2014), 16

Writer, speaker, and author Stasi Eldredge leads the women's ministry of Ransomed Heart and is the author of *Becoming Myself* and other titles especially for women. She blogs at RansomedHeart.com/blogs/Stasi.

Illustrated and hand-lettered by Laura Elizabeth Marshall

"Be joyful always; pray continually; give thanks in all circumstances, for this is God's will for you in Christ Jesus." —1 Thessalonians 5:16–18

Illustrated by Katherine Howe

WE WILL STAND *amazed* TO SEE THE TOPSIDE OF THE *tapestry* AND HOW GOD BEAUTIFULLY EMBROIDERED EACH CIRCUMSTANCE INTO A PATTERN FOR OUR GOOD AND HIS *glory*.

JONI EARECKSON TADA

"We will stand amazed to see the topside of the tapestry and how God beautifully embroidered each circumstance into a pattern for our good and His glory." —From *Heaven* by Joni Eareckson Tada (Grand Rapids: Zondervan, 1995)

Joni Eareckson Tada is an inspiration to millions. Becoming a quadriplegic after a diving accident in 1967 motivated her to help others in similar situations. She is an accomplished artist, prolific author, and the founder and CEO of Joni and Friends International Disability Center. She blogs at JoniAndFriends.org/blog/.

Illustrated and hand-lettered by Ann-Margret Hovsepian

you are altogether
BEAUTIFUL

SONG
OF
SOLOMON
4:7

"You are altogether beautiful, my love;
there is no flaw in you." —Song of Solomon 4:7 (ESV)

Illustrated and hand-lettered by Cari Logston

"God measures our entire existence by only two things: how we love Him and how we love people."
—From *For the Love* by Jen Hatmaker (Nashville: Thomas Nelson, 2015), 71

Jen Hatmaker and her husband, Brandon, pastor Austin New Church in Texas. Jen is a speaker, best-selling author, and star of the television series *My Big Family Renovation* on HGTV. Find Jen's blog at JenHatmaker.com.

Illustrated and hand-lettered by Jennifer Tucker

WE DON'T REALLY MAKE **FRIENDS,** THEY MAKE US.

BOB GOFF

"We don't really make friends, they make us." —Bob Goff

Attorney Bob Goff is the author of the best-selling book *Love Does*. He is also the founder of Restore International, a nonprofit human rights organization operating in Uganda, India, and Somalia. Follow Bob at BobGoff.com.

Illustrated and hand-lettered by Ann-Margret Hovsepian

"In peace I will both lie down and sleep;
for you alone, O LORD, make me dwell in safety." —Psalm 4:8 (ESV)

Illustrated and hand-lettered by Holly Camp

WE SEE THE

sacred

IN THE

ordinary.

SOPHIE · HUDSON

"As we share our stories with those people God has specifically ordained to walk with us on this side of eternity—and as they share their stories with us— we see the sacred in the ordinary. We see the profound in the mundane. We see the joy in the day to day." —From *A Little Salty to Cut the Sweet* by Sophie Hudson (Carol Stream, IL: Tyndale, 2013), 184

Blogger, author, and speaker Sophie Hudson loves to laugh and to help women find encouragement and hope in the everyday, joy-filled moments of life. Follow her at BooMama.net.

Illustrated and hand-lettered by Laura Elizabeth Marshall

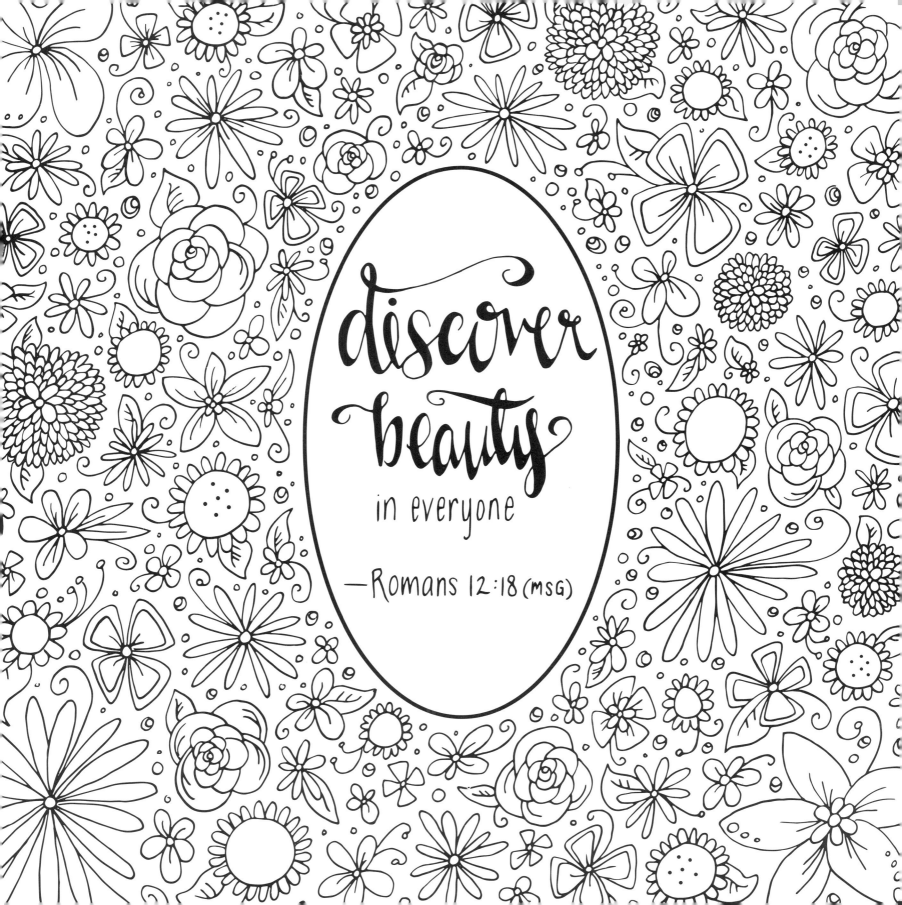

discover
beauty
in everyone

—Romans 12:18 (MSG)

"Bless your enemies; no cursing under your breath. Laugh with your happy friends when they're happy; share tears when they're down. Get along with each other; don't be stuck-up. Make friends with nobodies; don't be the great somebody.

"Don't hit back; discover beauty in everyone. If you've got it in you, get along with everybody. Don't insist on getting even; that's not for you to do. 'I'll do the judging,' says God. 'I'll take care of it.'" —Romans 12:14–19 (MSG)

Illustrated and hand-lettered by Holly Camp

Some of us are meant to be misfits....

Thank God for that. —Nish Weiseth

"Some of us are meant to be misfits....

"Thank God for that." —Nish Weiseth, from the blog
post "Misfit," October 23, 2013, at NishWeiseth.com

Nish Weiseth is the author of the book *Speak*. She speaks at churches, women's
groups, conferences, youth groups, and more across the country.

Illustrated by Katherine Howe

For the BEAUTY of the earth, FOR THE GLORY OF THE skies.

—FOLLIOTT S. PIERPOINT

## For the Beauty of the Earth
by Folliott S. Pierpoint

For the beauty of the earth,
For the glory of the skies,
For the love which from our birth
Over and around us lies.

*Refrain*

*Lord of all, to Thee we raise*
*This our hymn of grateful praise.*

For the beauty of each hour
Of the day and of the night,
Hill and vale, and tree and flower,
Sun and moon, and stars of light.

*Refrain*

For the joy of ear and eye,
For the heart and mind's delight,
For the mystic harmony
Linking sense to sound and sight.

*Refrain*

For the joy of human love,
Brother, sister, parent, child,
Friends on earth and friends above,
For all gentle thoughts and mild.

*Refrain*

For Thy Church, that evermore
Lifteth holy hands above,
Offering up on every shore
Her pure sacrifice of love.

*Refrain*

For the martyrs' crown of light,
For Thy prophets' eagle eye,
For Thy bold confessors' might,
For the lips of infancy.

*Refrain*

For Thy virgins' robes of snow,
For Thy maiden mother mild,
For Thyself, with hearts aglow,
Jesu, Victim undefiled.

*Refrain*

For each perfect Gift of Thine,
To our race so freely given,
Graces human and Divine,
Flowers of earth, and buds of Heaven.

*Refrain*

Folliott Pierpoint wrote this hymn in 1864 in reverence of the splendor of the surrounding countryside. The beautiful hymn was sung in the 1994 *Little Women* movie.

Illustrated and hand-lettered by Cari Logston

Dear one,
YOU'RE NOT BEING CONDEMNED.
YOU'RE BEING
rescued.
—Sarah Bessey

"You, dear one, you're not being condemned. You're being rescued." —Sarah Bessey, from the blog post "I Used to Think God Wanted a Lot from Me," July 7, 2015, at SarahBessey.com

A storyteller at heart, Sarah Bessey is an award-winning blogger, speaker, and author of the books *Out of Sorts* and *Jesus Feminist*.

Illustrated and hand-lettered by Terra Cypher

"I will make a covenant of peace with them and rid the land of wild beasts so that they may live in the desert and sleep in the forests in safety. I will bless them and the places surrounding my hill. I will send down showers in season; there will be showers of blessing. The trees of the field will yield their fruit and the ground will yield its crops; the people will be secure in their land. They will know that I am the LORD, when I break the bars of their yoke and rescue them from the hands of those who enslaved them. They will no longer be plundered by the nations, nor will wild animals devour them. They will live in safety, and no one will make them afraid. I will provide for them a land renowned for its crops, and they will no longer be victims of famine in the land or bear the scorn of the nations. Then they will know that I, the LORD their God, am with them and that they, the house of Israel, are my people, declares the Sovereign LORD. You my sheep, the sheep of my pasture, are people, and I am your God, declares the Sovereign LORD." —Ezekiel 34:25–31

Illustrated and hand-lettered by Ann-Margret Hovsepian

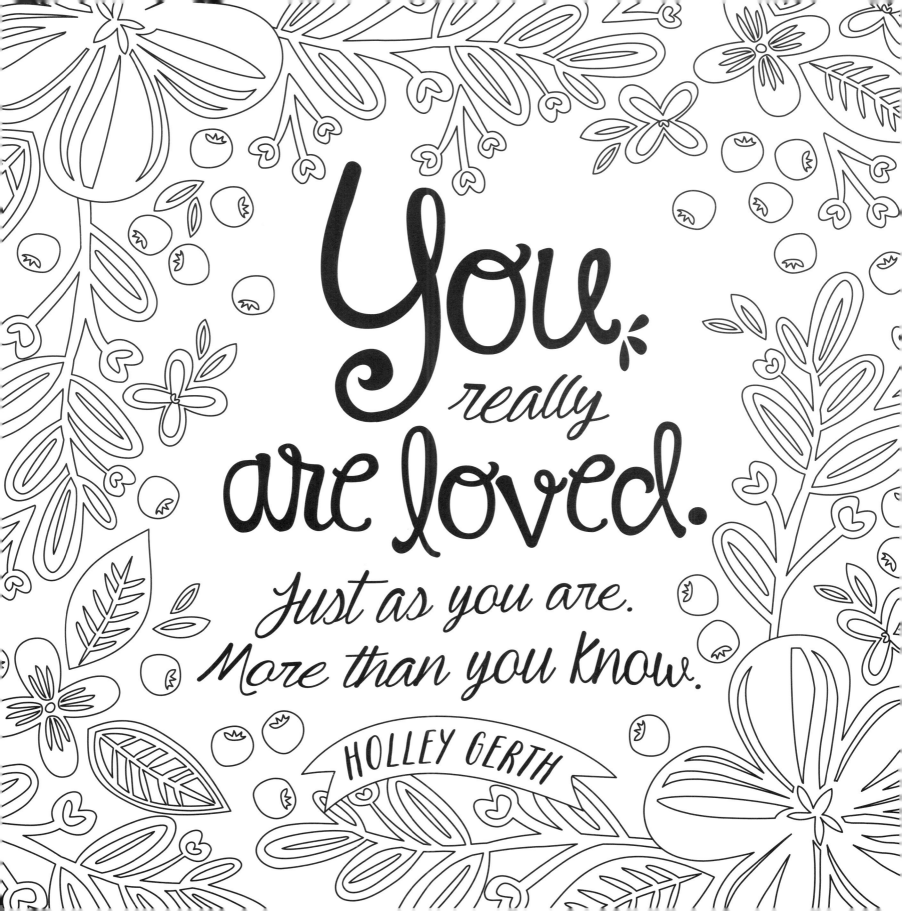

"You really are loved.

"Just as you are.

"More than you know.

"There's nothing that can change that in your life. Not a bad day, not a mistake, not all the ways you may sometimes worry you fall short. *Nothing*. So close your eyes, take a deep breath, and let the words wrap themselves around your heart." —Holley Gerth, from the blog post "You're Loved {Coffee for Your Heart}," January 15, 2014, at HolleyGerth.com

Holley Gerth is a best-selling writer, licensed counselor, certified life coach, and speaker. She is the co-founder of (in)courage and served as a writer and editorial director for DaySpring for over a decade. She is the author of more than a half-dozen books, including the best-selling *You're Already Amazing*.

Illustrated by Jenny Stewart

The heavens declare the glory of God, and the sky above proclaims his handiwork.

—Psalm 19:1 (ESV)

"The heavens declare the glory of God,
and the sky above proclaims his handiwork." —Psalm 19:1 (ESV)

Illustrated by Katherine Howe

ALL THINGS
bright
&
beautiful

—CECIL F. ALEXANDER

## All Things Bright and Beautiful
### By Cecil F. Alexander

*Refrain*

*All things bright and beautiful,*
*All creatures great and small,*
*All things wise and wonderful:*
*The Lord God made them all.*

Each little flower that opens,
Each little bird that sings,
He made their glowing colors,
He made their tiny wings.

*Refrain*

The purple-headed mountain,
The river running by,
The sunset and the morning
That brightens up the sky.

*Refrain*

The cold wind in the winter,
The pleasant summer sun,
The ripe fruits in the garden:
He made them every one.

*Refrain*

The tall trees in the greenwood,
The meadows where we play,
The rushes by the water,
To gather every day.

*Refrain*

He gave us eyes to see them,
And lips that we might tell
How great is God Almighty,
Who has made all things well.

*Refrain*

Cecil Frances Alexander wrote this hymn in 1848, based on Genesis 1:31 ("God saw all that he had made, and it was very good").

Illustrated by Jenny Stewart

mercy, peace and love be yours in abundance

—Jude 2

"To those who have been called, who are loved by
God the Father and kept by Jesus Christ:

"Mercy, peace and love be yours in abundance." —Jude 1–2

"Our God is the creator of the minuscule as well as the majestic." —Becky Wade

Becky Wade is the Carol Award, INSPY Award, and Inspirational Reader's Choice Award–winning author of the contemporary Christian romances *My Stubborn Heart, Undeniably Yours, Meant to Be Mine, A Love Like Ours,* and *Her One and Only.*

Illustrated and hand-lettered by Ann-Margret Hovsepian

I AM fearfully AND wonderfully made.

—PSALM 139:14 (ESV)

"For you created my inmost being;
        you knit me together in my mother's womb.
I praise you because I am fearfully and wonderfully made;
        your works are wonderful,
        I know that full well.
My frame was not hidden from you
        when I was made in the secret place.
When I was woven together in the depths of the earth,
        your eyes saw my unformed body.
All the days ordained for me
        were written in your book
        before one of them came to be.

How precious to me are your thoughts, O God!
        How vast is the sum of them!
Were I to count them,
        they would outnumber the grains of sand.
When I awake,
        I am still with you." —Psalm 139:13–18

Illustrated and hand-lettered by Jennifer Tucker

Give to the winds thy fears.

-Paul Gerhardt-

## Give to the Winds Thy Fears
### by Paul Gerhardt

Give to the winds thy fears;
Hope and be undismayed;
God hears thy sighs and counts thy tears,
God shall lift up thy head.

Through waves and clouds and storms,
He gently clears thy way;
Wait thou His time; so shall this night
Soon end in joyous day.

Still heavy is thy heart?
Still sinks thy spirit down?
Cast off the world, let fear depart,
Bid every care begone.

What though Thou rulest not;
Yet heaven, and earth, and hell
Proclaim, God sitteth on the throne,
And ruleth all things well.

And whatsoe'er Thou will'st,
Thou dost, O King of kings;

What Thine unerring wisdom chose,
Thy power to being brings.

Leave to His sovereign sway
To choose and to command;
So shalt thou, wondering, own His way,
How wise, how strong His hand.

Far, far above thy thought
His counsel shall appear,
When fully He the work hath wrought
That caused thy needless fear.

Thou seest our weakness, Lord;
Our hearts are known to Thee;
O lift Thou up the sinking hand,
Confirm the feeble knee!

Let us in life, in death,
Thy steadfast truth declare,
And publish with our latest breath
Thy love and guardian care.

This hymn, written in German by Paul Gerhardt in 1656 and translated to English in 1737 by John Wesley, complements Psalm 34:4 ("I sought the Lord, and he answered me; he delivered me from all my fears").

Illustrated and hand-lettered by Terra Cypher

I have learned THE secret of being content in any AND every situation.

—PHILIPPIANS 4:12

"I know what it is to be in need, and I know what it is to have plenty. I have learned the secret of being content in any and every situation, whether well fed or hungry, whether living in plenty or in want. I can do everything through him who gives me strength."
—Philippians 4:12–13

Illustrated and hand-lettered by Laura Elizabeth Marshall

Blessed are all who take refuge in him.

—Psalm 2:12

"Blessed are all who take refuge in him." —Psalm 2:12

Illustrated and hand-lettered by Holly Camp

The beauty of His creation points to the beauty of Him.

—Liz Curtis Higgs

"The beauty of His creation points to the beauty of Him." —Liz Curtis Higgs, from the blog post "The One Who Names the Stars," July 16, 2015, at LizCurtisHiggs.com

Liz Curtis Higgs is the author of more than thirty books with 4.5 million copies in print, including her nonfiction bestsellers *Bad Girls of the Bible, The Girl's Still Got It,* and *The Women of Christmas*, and her Scottish historical novels *Here Burns My Candle* and *Mine Is the Night*. Liz has spoken at more than 1,700 women's conferences around the world.

Illustrated and hand-lettered by Lisa Shirk

Consider the lilies, HOW THEY GROW: THEY NEITHER toil NOR spin.

—Luke 12:27 (ESV)

"Consider the lilies, how they grow: they neither toil nor spin, yet I tell you, even Solomon in all his glory was not arrayed like one of these. But if God so clothes the grass, which is alive in the field today, and tomorrow is thrown into the oven, how much more will he clothe you, O you of little faith! And do not seek what you are to eat and what you are to drink, nor be worried. For all the nations of the world seek after these things, and your Father knows that you need them. Instead, seek his kingdom, and these things will be added to you."
—Luke 12:27–31 (ESV)

Illustrated and hand-lettered by Jennifer Tucker

"We are made of love and all the beauty stemming
from it." —From the song "Needle and Thread,"
written by Ryan O'Neal of the band Sleeping at Last

Sleeping at Last is the moniker of Chicago-based singer-songwriter, producer, and
composer, Ryan O'Neal. Sleeping at Last can be heard frequently on popular TV
shows and films such as *The Twilight Saga: Breaking Dawn—Part 1*, *The Fault in
Our Stars* trailer, *Grey's Anatomy*, *So You Think You Can Dance*, *Criminal Minds*,
*Bones*, *The Vampire Diaries*, and J. J. Abrams and Alfonso Cuaron's *Believe*.

Illustrated and hand-lettered by Laura Elizabeth Marshall

## ILLUSTRATORS AND HAND-LETTERERS

We'd like to give a big thank-you to the following nine people for sharing their creativity on the pages of this book. We handed them the text and set them loose to illustrate it in their own unique styles. You can check out their websites and Etsy sites to see more of their art and learn more about them.

Holly Camp (HollyCampCards.etsy.com)
Terra Cypher (Etsy.com/shop/WildGoatDesign)
Ann-Margret Hovsepian (AnnHovsepian.com)
Katherine Howe (KatiesInkyInspirations.Wordpress.com)
Cari Logston (SunLettering.com)
Laura Elizabeth Marshall (Etsy.com/shop/DoodlingForDays)
Lisa Shirk (LisaShirk.com)
Jenny Stewart (FrenchPressMornings.com)
Jennifer Tucker (LittleHouseStudio.net)

## WATERBROOK

Thank you to all of the individuals and departments within the Crown Division and WaterBrook for their help in creating this project—in particular Lori Addicott, Laura Barker, Candice Chaplin, Tina Constable, Christine Edwards, Alex Field, Bridget Givan, Ginia Hairston Croker, Debbie Mitchell, Andrew Rein, Beverly Rykerd, Sara Selkirk, and Julia Wallace. A very special thank-you to Karen Sherry, Pam Fogle, and Lynn Sheppard for their time and talent in the design and typesetting process.

## *EVERYTHING BEAUTIFUL* DEVELOPMENT TEAM

Kendall Davis
Jessica Gingrich
Amy Haddock
Jessica Lamb
Susan Tjaden

## PLAYLIST

We truly want this book to help you engage in a rich worship experience and to be uplifting to your soul and spirit. Music speaks so much deeper than just words, so we've created a playlist of songs to listen to while you create your unique work of art. We know the result will be beautiful.

https://open.spotify.com/user/waterbrookmultnomah
Playlist: "Everything Beautiful"

# COLOR YOUR WAY TO PEACE & WORSHIP